This Book Belongs To:

ISBN 13: 978-1-4621-4736-6
ebook ISBN 13: 978-1-4621-4780-9

Published by CFI, an imprint of Cedar Fort, Inc.
2373 W. 700 S., Suite 100, Springville, UT 84663
Distributed by Cedar Fort, Inc., www.cedarfort.com

Cover design by Angela Smith and Shawnda T. Craig

Edited by Sarina Betts
Typeset by Sarina Betts and Shawnda T. Craig
Printed in the United States of America

10 9 8 7 6 5 4 3 2 1

Printed on acid-free paper

Becoming a Woman of God

A 6-Week Study Journal

Seeking Diligently

CFI
An imprint of Cedar Fort, Inc.
Springville, Utah

Contents

A Letter from the Author vii

Meet the Author, Rachel Rhien Tucker viii

Meet the Artist, Angela Smith ix

Week One - Personal Conversion 1

Week Two - Strengthening Faith 13

Week Three - Different from the World 23

Week Four - Finding Your Purpose 33

Week Five - Ministry and Service 43

Week Six - Sharing His Light 51

Moving Forward 59

Reflect and Review 61

References 67

A Letter to You

My dear friend,

You are a child of God. You have specific, divine traits and characteristics that came directly from your heavenly parents. You are like them. You share their spiritual DNA. They created you—unique and beautiful—and sent you to earth at this time for a specific purpose. They've given you wonderful and amazing gifts that will help you draw closer to the Savior, and will aid you in sharing the light of His gospel with others.

You have a divine mission to fulfill, and while sometimes it may seem that life is muddy and it's hard to know what that mission is, as you strengthen your testimony, search the scriptures, and seek for personal revelation through focused and heartfelt prayer, you will come to realize your great purpose and potential.

You are an essential part of this ongoing Restoration, and the Lord needs you. He needs your talents, He needs your personality, He needs your intellect and your testimony. He needs you to shine His light for the world to see. You are exactly where you're supposed to be, and the lessons that you're learning in this season will be a gift and a blessing not only to you, but to your family and friends, and those who need your love and empathy.

Take time each day to be quiet. Take time to think, reflect, and listen. Give your spirit the love and attention it needs. As you focus on the fundamentals in your life, as you cut out the frivolous things that take up your time and mental energy, as you pray to know where God needs you each day, you will be blessed with the opportunity to change hearts and lives, starting with your own.

Thank you for showing up. Thank you for "seeking diligently."

You are incredible.

Rachel

Meet the Author

Rachel Rhien Tucker is a wife and mother of four who lives in Southern California. Rachel graduated from Northern Arizona University and earned a Bachelor's degree in Spanish. She has lived in a number of different countries and continues to value the education that comes with travel. Rachel is the owner and CEO of Seeking Diligently, where she is a writer and public speaker. Rachel has spoken at many women's conferences and hosted her own gathering, Arise Conference, in 2023. She is excited about the prospect of expanding that conference to new areas.

Rachel is most in her element when teaching or writing about the gospel of Jesus Christ. She taught early-morning seminary for 5 years and loves teaching others how to apply the scriptures to their lives. Rachel writes a daily devotional on Instagram and can be found @seeking_diligently.

Meet the Artist

Angela Smith is a wife, mother, and artist based in Utah. She was born in Oahu, Hawaii and adopted as a baby.

Angela was surrounded by talented artists growing up, including her mother, but didn't pursue art seriously until 2020 at the age of twenty-six. She started her business during the pandemic and has loved creating for herself and others.

She is a firm believer that anybody can and should create.

Angela is African American/Polynesian. Being a minority in Utah has heavily influenced her art and she loves creating pieces that depict women and people of color. Inclusive culture is very important to her because being different isn't easy and embracing other cultures and differences is something we should all strive for.

Angela has a selection of religious art. She is known for her watercolor florals which she creates both traditionally and in a digital medium.

Angela loves hiking, reading, and spending time with her husband and children.

Week One

Personal Conversion

Discipleship, in any form, must start with personal conversion to the Savior and His gospel. The word "conversion" comes from "convert," which means to change into another form or state; to adapt to a new or different purpose. Conversion then, in its simplest form, means to change. It means that we leave what we once were to become something new, to grow toward a different purpose.

As we diligently seek to become women of God, we will start to notice these changes in ourselves. We will find ourselves drawn to things that nourish our spirits. We will have a deep desire to live our lives for a different, holier purpose. We will begin to notice all of the ways and places that Jesus Christ shows up in our daily lives. And we will allow those experiences, no matter how small, to nourish our ongoing conversion to Him and His gospel.

In the book *True to the Faith*, we read that "conversion is a process, not an event. You become converted as a result of . . . righteous efforts to follow the Savior." Our personal conversion grows day by day as we spend time in heartfelt prayer, study God's word through the scriptures and living prophets, and seek to become more like the Savior.

Jesus Christ's gospel is a gospel of change, and repentance is the most beautiful avenue to change that we can experience. There is perhaps nothing that will draw us closer to our Savior more quickly than approaching Him with a sincere and repentant heart. As we utilize the incomparable gifts of His Atonement in our lives, as we turn away from those things that keep us from Him and turn toward His outstretched arms, we will feel deep personal conversion growing within our souls, and we will experience the mighty change of heart defined in Mosiah 5:2 as "[having] no more disposition to the evil, but to do good continually."

Personal Affirmation:

As I seek to deepen my conversion to Jesus Christ every day
and use the power of His mighty Atonement in my life,
He draws me close and empowers me to choose Him.

Personal Conversion

Study 1

DAILY READING:

"He Knows You By Name," by Elaine S. Dalton
April 2005 General Conference

Joseph Smith History 1:13 • James 1:5 • Isaiah 40:26

Q: God spoke to many different scriptural characters and called them by name. Have you ever had that experience? When? Read your patriarchal blessing this week and look for every time the Lord shows that He knows you by name (if you haven't received it yet, prayerfully consider doing so).

Q: At the age of 14, young Joseph Smith established a pattern that we can follow to gain and strengthen our testimonies. What do you need clarity on right now? What answers are you seeking? Study James 1:5 and ask God. Receiving answers may require time and patience, but the answers will come.

Q: Sister Dalton speaks of angels who help us. Who are your heavenly angels? Who are your earthly angels? How have you seen God's hand in your life through them?

Personal Conversion

Study 2

DAILY READING:

"The Soul's Sincere Desire," by Carol F. McConkie
October 2016 General Conference

Luke 18:1-8 • Matthew 7:7-11 • Jacob 3:1-2

Q: Heavenly Father deeply values our communication with Him. He wants to hear from you and He wants to speak to you. When we receive answers to our prayers, it's essential that we act on the inspiration we receive. When have you responded in faith to promptings you've received, even when they felt scary or didn't make sense? Can you see now the blessings that came from that act of faith?

Q: Sister McConkie warns against using repetition in our prayers. How can you strive to be more present and mindful when you pray? What specific things can you do to make every prayer you offer personal and meaningful?

Invitation:

Create a habit of offering prayers of only gratitude and thanksgiving. As you do so, your eyes will be opened to the generous gifts that Father in Heaven has granted you. He will recognize your gratitude and continue to bless you with those things you need and desire.

Personal Conversion

Study 3

DAILY READING:

"Trust in the Lord and Lean Not," by Bonnie H. Cordon
April 2017 General Conference

2 Nephi 22:2 • Mosiah 1:6-7 • Mosiah 7:33

Q: Sister Cordon discusses what it means to lean spiritually, to get off center, and lose our balance. Are there things in your life that you find yourself "leaning on your own understanding" for? What are they? How can you courageously hand those things back over to the Lord and trust Him with them?

Q: As you come to trust the Lord, you will start to see His hand in your life more clearly. Sister Cordon mentions three things to focus on as we learn to trust more deeply in the Savior: scripture study, prayer, and service. How can you improve in one or all of these areas?

Invitation:

–Keep a current problem or concern in your mind as you study your scriptures. Look for ways that the Lord speaks to you about those specific things you're struggling with.

–Pray to know who needs your help. Pray for opportunities to serve others. Peace and enlightenment will come to you as you extend yourself and share Christ's love and light.

Personal Conversion

Study 4

DAILY READING:

"God's Love: The Most Joyous to the Soul," by Susan H. Porter
October 2021 General Conference

1 Nephi 11:16-17 • Moroni 7:47-48 • Jeremiah 31:3

Q: Sister Porter teaches, "Sometimes we mistakenly think that we can feel God's love only after we have followed the iron rod and partaken of the fruit. God's love, however, not only is received by those who come to the tree but is the very power that motivates us to seek that tree." How does the Lord's love for you individually help motivate you to seek Him? In what ways can you make that a more constant goal in your life?

Q: The Lord honors the questions that we ask. He wants to give us insights and answers, but those things don't always come quickly. What are the questions that you have? How can you continue to move forward while searching for answers?

Q: In Moroni 7:48, Mormon asks us to pray that we might know of God's love for us. When have you felt God's love for you as one of His unique and essential daughters? If you haven't felt it lately, ask Him to bless you to know how He feels about you.

Personal Conversion

Study 5

DAILY READING:

"Be Ye Converted," by Bonnie L. Oscarson
October 2013 General Conference

Mosiah 5:2 • Luke 22:3 • John 7:17

Q: What does true, individual, personal conversion mean to you? How can you deepen your conversion to Jesus Christ and His gospel?

Q: Sister Oscarson teaches that true conversion begins to take place when we have faithfully lived a gospel principle, after which the Spirit testifies to our hearts that the principle is good and true. What is something you feel you would like a deeper testimony of, and what steps can you take in faith to invite the Spirit to teach you of its truth?

Notes

Week Two

Strengthening Faith

We live in a dark and fallen world. It is a world of cynicism, criticism, and for many people, unbelief. Not only is there a lack of faith, but many people struggle to have hope as well. Faith and hope go hand in hand. Indeed, it is quite difficult to have great faith without also having great hope (See Alma 32:21 and Hebrews 11:1).

Another important aspect to faith is trust. Hope + trust = faith. Do we have hope in Jesus Christ? Do we trust Him? If the answer to those questions is yes, even if it's a hesitant yes, then faith is present. Strengthening our faith comes as we increase our hope and our trust in Him.

Perhaps this involves learning more about our Savior and His life. Perhaps it involves studying His word more regularly. Perhaps it involves cultivating a habit of daily repentance. No matter the steps we start with, each one is important in deepening our faith. The Lord loves effort, and He rewards it graciously. If our goal each day is to seek Him, to come closer to and become more like Him, then our faith will automatically get stronger.

Mosiah 57 reads, "And now, because of the covenant which ye have made ye shall be called the children of Christ, his sons, and his daughters; for behold, this day he hath spiritually begotten you; for ye say that your hearts are changed through faith on his name; therefore, ye are born of him and have become his sons and his daughters."

Conversion is change, and change comes through faith. When we fix our hearts on the Savior, when we increase our hope and trust in Him, when we humble ourselves before Him, "then will [He] make weak things become strong unto [us]" (Ether 12:27).

Personal Affirmation:

I am known and loved by my Savior.
I trust in Him, and I trust Him.
My hope and faith in Him grows as I seek Him each day.

Strengthening Faith

Study 1

DAILY READING:

"Fear Not, I Am with Thee," by Jean A. Stevens
April 2014 General Conference

Alma 37:37 • Moses 1:39 • Isaiah 41:10

Q: When have you felt the hand of the Lord in your life? When has He answered your prayers? Take a few moments and jot down your experiences. Remembering when He has helped you in the past will strengthen your faith that He hears your prayers and that He will, in His own time, bless you with the answers that you seek.

Q: "Tender mercies" from the Lord aren't always big events. Most of the time, they're small things that we can overlook if we're not mindful. Thinking over the past week, make a list of the tender mercies that you or your family were blessed with. How can you be more mindful of and grateful for the ways that the Lord shows up for you?

Strengthening Faith

Study 2

DAILY READING:

"Be of a Good Courage," by Ann M. Dibb
April 2010 General Conference

Joshua 1:5-8 • Isaiah 40:31

Q: Having faith often takes courage. At the same time, courage is strengthened as we exercise faith. What is something you're facing right now that requires courage? What daily decisions can you make that will strengthen your courage and faith?

Q: Sister Dibb teaches us from the story of Joshua in the Old Testament about four guides: prayer, obedience to God's commandments, daily scripture study, and a commitment to follow the living prophet. Which of those four areas could use some extra attention in your own life?

Strengthening Faith

Study 3

DAILY READING:

"A Woman of Faith," by Margaret D. Nadauld
October 2002 General Conference

Alma 5:14 • Doctrine & Covenants 112:10 • Psalm 23:4

Q: In what ways have you been fearless in your faith? In what ways do you desire to be more fearless in your faith, and how can you achieve them?

Q: Thinking about your children or others you may have influence over, how can you help them increase their faith? What can you share with them that will positively impact their belief in loving heavenly parents and a Savior who knows them personally?

Q: How can you share your faith more openly with all you come in contact with in your daily life?

Strengthening Faith

Study 4

DAILY READING:

"Believe!" by Elaine S. Dalton
April 2004 General Conference

2 Nephi 32:9 • Doctrine & Covenants 64:33 • 1 Timothy 4:12

Q: President Gordon B. Hinckley stated, "I believe in my capacity and in your capacity to do good, to make some contribution to the society of which we are a part, to grow and develop, and to do things that we may now think are impossible" ("I Believe"). Make a list of your God-given strengths. What are ways that you know you can use them to make a difference in the lives of others?

Q: There are times, even as an adult, when you may feel that you are standing alone. But you are never alone. Who are the people in your life that you can lean on for support and solidarity? Who can you trust with the things of your heart, with your convictions and with your beliefs? Turn to those people and strengthen those relationships. Then determine that you're going to be that steady, non-judgmental person for others.

Q: When have you experienced the blessing of finding answers to your questions or problems in the scriptures? How have those experiences shaped your testimony of the importance of the written word of God?

Strengthening Faith

Study 5

DAILY READING:

"Seeing the Promises Afar Off," by Anne C. Pingree
October 2003 General Conference

Doctrine & Covenants 123:17 • Mark 9:23 • James 1:6

Q: "Faith" and "hope" are complementary but have different meanings. What do each of these words mean to you? How can you use one to strengthen the other?

Q: Sister Pingree defines faith as "the spiritual ability to be persuaded of promises that are seen 'afar off.'" With that definition in mind, what things in your personal life are "afar off" and require extra faith from you right now? How can you cultivate the faith needed to confidently await those things?

Notes

Week Three

Different From the World

The world is very good at telling us who we are and who we're not. The adversary thrives on distracting us from our divine missions and causing us to forget who we are. Comparison is everywhere and it takes very little to get sucked into the habit of picking ourselves apart and focusing on what we lack. But that behavior is detrimental to our mental health as well as our spiritual growth and potential.

The Lord thrives on reminding us who we really are: daughters of heavenly parents with a divine heritage and destiny. Remembering our true identity and helping others come to that knowledge is one of the most important things we can concentrate on in this life.

"Now it is for you and for me to carry forward the banner into the next century. We are not women of the world. We are women of God. And women of God will be among the greatest heroines of the 21st century. As President Joseph F. Smith proclaimed, 'it is not for us to be led by the women of the world; it is for [us] to lead . . . the women of the world, in everything that is praise-worthy'" (Sheri L. Dew, "We Are Women of God").

It's time to get rid of the things in our lives that only serve to distract and derail us from our most important personal missions. It's time to abandon anything that makes us question our worth and potential. We must remember who we are! We must not forget who we were created to become. We must be different from the world in order to help change the world. It's only when we do this that we can fully become an instrument in the hands of the Lord and fulfill our divine purposes.

Personal Affirmation:

I am a daughter of God and was sent to earth
with a divine mission to fulfill. I do not allow
the world to distract me or diminish my worth.

Different from the World

Study 1

DAILY READING:

"Certain Women," by Linda K. Burton
April 2017 General Conference

Luke 8:1-3 • John 11:21-27 • Esther 4:13-16

Q: Sister Burton lists a few synonyms for the word "certain" in the context of faithful women: "convinced," "positive," "confident," "firm," "definite," "assured," and "dependable." Which of these traits do you feel you possess? Which of these traits would you like to develop on a deeper level?

Q: The scriptures teach us that becoming a "certain" woman and a covenant-keeping disciple requires our willingness to sacrifice. What are the sacrifices that you make as a "certain" woman and disciple of Christ? Is there something else you can give to deepen your commitment to the Savior?

Q: When considering Jesus Christ, what are you certain about?

Different from the World

Study 2

DAILY READING:

"Live According to the Words of the Prophets," by Carol F. McConkie
October 2014 General Conference

Mosiah 2:9 • 3 Nephi 20:23-25 • Proverbs 3:5

Q: Sister McConkie recounts the story of Elijah the prophet and Zarephath, a poor widow trying to feed her son. Elijah asked her for water and food, and she faithfully obliged (1 Kings 17). When have you been asked to do something by the prophet that has required you to exercise faith? How were you blessed for doing so?

Q: How has studying the words of modern prophets and other leaders of the Church sustained you through difficult times?

Q: How have the words of modern prophets and other leaders of the Church strengthened your testimony of Jesus Christ?

Different from the World

Study 3

DAILY READING:

"Press Forward and Be Steadfast," by Elaine S. Dalton
April 2003 General Conference

2 Nephi 31:20 • 2 Nephi 32:5 • 1 Kings 19:12

Q: Sister Dalton notes in her talk that "each of you will experience resistance from worldly forces." What are some things in your own life that blow fiercely against you? What does it mean to you to be firmly planted in your faith, and how can you strengthen yourself against opposition?

Q: How can daily concerted scripture study and heartfelt personal prayer help you to be steadfast and immovable? How can they help you make choices that will lead you back to the Savior?

Different from the World

Study 4

DAILY READING:

"Stay on the Path," by Elaine S. Dalton
April 2007 General Conference

Doctrine & Covenants 25:2,10,13,15 • Psalm 23:3

Q: What personal moral standards do you have that help you to be virtuous? The word "modesty" has a number of different meanings. What does the word mean to you? How can you implement modesty in your life to come closer to God?

Q: When have you been able to influence others for good by bravely and confidently living your faith? How have you been positively influenced by others who live their faith?

Different from the World

Study 5

DAILY READING:

"An Especially Noble Calling," by Joy D. Jones
April 2020 General Conference

Doctrine & Covenants 58:26-28 • 2 Nephi 9:39-42

Q: Sister Jones, in talking about the powerful influence of women, quotes the Prophet Joseph Smith, who counseled the sisters to "live up to [their] privilege." What does it mean to you, as a covenant daughter of God living in these important times, to "live up to your privileges?"

Q: Think carefully about the covenants you've made in your life. How do your covenants set you apart from the world? How have you felt the power of God in your life as you've honored and held tight to those covenants?

Notes

Week Four

Finding Your Purpose

You are unique. You have divine gifts, traits, and talents that you were given for a specific purpose. You are capable of more than you can imagine, and you were made "for such a time as this" (Esther 4:14). You, my friend, are right where you're supposed to be. Alma 26:3 reads, "This is the blessing which hath been bestowed upon us, that we have been made instruments in the hands of God to bring about this great work."

When your spirit was created by mindful and loving heavenly parents, They gave you distinct spiritual gifts that will allow you to be successful in fulfilling your divine role. You have a specific purpose and a mission to fulfill. But how does one go about discovering what that is? It helps to start by recognizing your gifts. What do those things with which you've been endowed teach you about what your mission may be? What comes easily to you? How can you use those gifts to bless the lives of your family and others?

Kathleen H. Hughes taught, "The Lord has touched my spirit time and again, and more often than not, His touch has reached me through the hand of a friend . . . Perhaps [we] would feel more of His love if [we] looked for His hand in the actions of those who care for [us] . . . God knows the needs of His children, and He often works through us, prompting us to help one another. When we act on such promptings, we tread on holy ground, for we are allowed the opportunity to serve as an agent of God in answering a prayer" ("What Greater Goodness Can We Know: Christlike Friends").

So begin today. Make a list of your strengths. Pray and ask for guidance and direction. Seek to understand your divine mission. As you do so, the Lord will guide you to know how you can be an instrument in His hands. He will point you toward those who need you and your gifts.

Personal Affirmation:

I have been blessed with specific gifts and traits by heavenly parents.
I have a divine mission to fulfill, and I seek the Lord's guidance as
I use my talents to serve those around me.

Finding Your Purpose

Study 1

DAILY READING:

"Divine Discontent," by Michelle D. Craig
October 2018 General Conference

James 1:5 • Philippians 4:13 • Hebrews 4:16

Q: Elder Neal A. Maxwell defined "divine discontent" as what results from comparing "what we are [to] what we have the power to become" ("Becoming a Disciple"). Coming to honestly recognize where we are lacking and how we can be better is essential to growing into the person God needs us to be. In what areas of your life do you feel "divine discontent"? What steps do you need to take to change?

Q: Sister Craig states that "our discontent can become divine — or destructive." How can you choose to let it lead you toward the Savior, rather than toward comparison and doubt? What steps can you take to believe more in yourself and in the power of the Atonement to help you master your life?

Q: Life is busy. Each day seems filled with lists of things to do, appointments to keep, places to be. How can you structure your days to ensure that you're *becoming* more and not just *doing* more?

Finding Your Purpose

Study 2

DAILY READING:

"Invite Christ to Author Your Story," by Camille N. Johnson
October 2021 General Conference

Moroni 6:4 • John 14:16-17 • Hebrews 12:2

Q: Sister Johnson quotes President Russell M. Nelson, who taught that we "receive more faith by doing something that requires more faith" ("Christ Is Risen; Faith in Him Will Move Mountains"). Have you experienced this? What is happening in your life right now that's requiring you to use more faith? Can you see your faith strengthening?

Q: Look back at the story of your life thus far. What were the plot twists? What lessons did they teach? What were the beautiful surprises? What can you do to more fully turn your life over to the Lord and allow Him to author your story?

Finding Your Purpose

Study 3

DAILY READING:

"And upon the Handmaids in Those Days
Will I Pour Out My Spirit," by Julie B. Beck
April 2010 General Conference

2 Nephi 32:3 • Doctrine & Covenants 11:12-14 • Joel 2:28-29

Q: Sister Beck notes that "being in the right places allows us to receive guidance." Sometimes, being in the "right places" doesn't mean being physically in the right places. Often it means being in the "right places" mentally and spiritually. How can you ensure that you're in the "right place" and ready to receive promptings from the Lord during your day?

Q: What questions are you seeking answers to right now? What can you do to strengthen your faith that you will receive those answers?

Finding Your Purpose

Study 4

DAILY READING:

"Spiritual Capacity," by Michelle Craig
October 2018 General Conference

1 Nephi 3:7 • Moroni 7:16 • Doctrine and Covenants 42:61

Q: Sister Craig encourages us to be intentional about creating time and space to hear God's voice. When can you set aside 15-20 minutes in your day to commune with your Heavenly Father? Do you need to wake up a little early, retreat to your closet for a few minutes in the afternoon, or sacrifice some screen time? Determine a specific time and place where you can sit in stillness and quietly seek out your own personal revelation.

Q: When have you felt an impression and immediately acted on it? What were the results of your actions? In contrast, when have you felt an impression and delayed action? How were those results different?

Q: You have traits and talents that make you uniquely equipped to help others and fulfill your personal mission. Which talents have our heavenly parents blessed you with? How can you use them to lift others and, in the process, be uplifted yourself?

Finding Your Purpose

Study 5

DAILY READING:

"Knowing the Lord's Will for You," by Anne C. Pingree
October 2005 General Conference

Alma 26:3 • 3 Nephi 18:20 • Doctrine & Covenants 9:8

Q: Sister Pingree quoted Neal A. Maxwell when he taught, "The submission of one's will is really the only uniquely personal thing we have to place on God's altar. It is the only possession which is truly ours to give!" ("Swallowed Up in the Will of the Father,"). Our free will is the only thing we have to give to God that He doesn't already possess. What can you do to show Him that you are seeking to more closely align your will with His?

Invitation:

Read your patriarchal blessing (if you haven't received it yet, prayerfully consider doing so). Look for the things in your blessing that perhaps haven't yet come to pass. Determine what you can do to faithfully submit your will to the Lord in regards to those things, and prayerfully work toward them.

Notes

Week Five

Ministry and Service

"You can recognize women who are grateful to be a daughter of God by their attitude. They know that the errand of angels is given to women, and they desire to be on God's errand to love His children and minister to them, to teach them the doctrines of salvation, to call them to repentance, to save them in perilous circumstances, to guide them in the performance of His work, to deliver His messages. They understand that they can bless their Father's children in their homes and neighborhoods and beyond. Women who are grateful to be daughters of God bring glory to His name" (Margaret D. Nadauld, "The Joy of Womanhood").

As women, we often fall into the trap of trying to do it all, shoulder it all, and fix it all. It's easy to multi-task to the point of exhaustion and failure. We cannot do all of the things, all of the time, and do them well. When we find ourselves out of balance in times like this, we need to prioritize and refocus on the most important things.

Our heavenly parents have given each one of us unique, divine spiritual gifts and abilities that serve three purposes: 1) to draw us closer to Them, 2) to help us on our mortal journey here on earth, and 3) to help others.

As we seek to know, understand, and develop the attributes and qualities that have been given to us, it's important that we own and claim them. Humility doesn't come as we hide our gifts, but as we eagerly and confidently use those gifts to lift and serve those around us. As we learn to use our talents to bless the lives of others, we will feel an abundance of the love that our Savior has for us and those we serve.

Personal Affirmation:

I have been given unique, divine gifts and talents that I use to praise God, strengthen myself, and serve others.

Ministry and Service

Study 1

DAILY READING:

"What Greater Goodness Can We Know:
Christlike Friends," by Kathleen H. Hughes
April 2005 General Conference

Doctrine & Covenants 81:5-6 • John 13:15 • Jude 1:20-22

Q: How have you felt the love that the Lord has for you through the actions of another person? How can you be an earthly angel for someone else?

Q: Do you know people who are on the margins at church, at work, or in your community? How can you show them genuine friendship and help them feel the love of the Lord?

Ministry and Service

Study 2

DAILY READING:

"The Needs before Us," by Bonnie L. Oscarson
October 2017 General Conference

Mosiah 18:9 • Proberbs 17:17 • D&C 38:27

Q: Sister Oscarson teaches that "some of the most significant needs we can meet are within our own families, among our friends, in our wards, and in our communities." When think of service, we usually think of big projects, but more often than not, we can do the most good closer to home. Who in your family needs special service today? Which of your friends could use a text that you're thinking of them? Which stranger at the grocery store would benefit from a smile and kind word?

Q: How can you make yourself more available for others (physically, spiritually, and emotionally)? What small things can you do to help others feel seen and heard?

Ministry and Service

Study 3

DAILY READING:

"For Him," by Joy D. Jones
October 2018 General Conference

Mosiah 2:17 • Alma 26:12 • Matthew 6:1-6, 33

Q: We all have people in our lives who are more difficult to love and serve than others. Who is that person for you? Perhaps it's an unfriendly neighbor, or someone you've had a falling out with, or even one of your own children. How can you shift your focus to God when it comes to loving and serving that person? How could doing so change the dynamic of your relationship?

Q: Sister Jones teaches that "we can make each item on our to-do list become a way to glorify Him." Think about your day today. What's on your list of things to get done? How can you do them in a way that glorifies God?

Ministry and Service

Study 4

DAILY READING:

"The Joy of Unselfish Service," by Christina B. Franco
October 2018 General Conference

Doctrine & Covenants 4:2 • Matthew 22:37, 39

Q: When have you been on the receiving end of heartfelt service? How were you able to see the hand of God through the service someone else gave you?

Q: When have you felt joy as you've served someone else? Can you think of specific examples?

Q: What can you sacrifice today to bless someone else's life? Convenience? Time? Money?

Ministry and Service

Study 5

DAILY READING:

"Cat's Cradle of Kindness," by Chieko Okazaki
April 1993 General Conference

Matthew 7:12 • Ephesians 4:32 • Colossians 2:2

Q: Is there a person who has played only a small role, but who left a beautiful thread in the tapestry that is your life? In the same way, how can you influence the lives of others for the better, even if your meeting is only momentary?

Q: Which of the Savior's attributes would you like to develop or strengthen as you seek to make your life more like His in regards to serving and loving others?

Notes

Week Six

Sharing His Light

Jesus Christ taught, "I am the light of the world: he that followeth me shall not walk in darkness, but shall have the light of life" (John 8:12). Interestingly, Matthew 5:14 teaches, "Ye are the light of the world." How can this be?

We are the light of the world because we've each been blessed with the light of Christ. It is a gift freely given to all who've been born on this earth. His light is within us. And we are to share it with the world.

Matthew 5:14-16 goes on to say, "A city that is set on an hill cannot be hid. Neither do men light a candle, and put it under a bushel, but on a candlestick; and it giveth light unto all that are in the house. Let your light so shine before men, that they may see your good works, and glorify your Father which is in heaven."

We've been given an incredible and exciting charge: to boldly live our faith and to share the light of Jesus Christ and His gospel with the world. We have beautiful examples from the scriptures of women who fulfilled this role: Mother Eve, Mary Magdalene, Mary the Mother of Jesus, Esther, Ruth, the mothers of the army of Helaman, and others.

May we emulate those brave women who dedicated their lives to reflecting His light. May we heed the Apostle Paul's words to Timothy: "Be thou an example of the believers, in word, in conversation, in charity, in spirit, in faith, in purity"(1 Timothy 4:12). May we each live our lives in a way that will cause others to want to know Him because they know us.

Personal Affirmation:

I live each day in a way that allows the light of Christ to radiate from me in all that I do. I honor Him by being like Him, and in doing so I help others to come to know Him as well.

Sharing His Light

Study 1

DAILY READING:

"Stand Tall and Stand Together," by Sheri Dew
October 2000 General Conference

1 Nephi 13:37 • Mosiah 18:8-9

Q: Have you ever encountered a complete stranger and somehow known that they shared your faith or values? What were the attributes you noticed that stood out in that person?

Q: Sister Dew reminds us, "For eons of time our Father watched us and knew He could trust us when so much would be at stake. We have been held in reserve for this very hour." He knows how strong His faithful daughters are! How does it make you feel, knowing that our Heavenly Father placed you right where you are, in this most crucial time, to do a specific work?

Sharing His Light

Study 2

DAILY READING:

"Charity Never Faileth," by Silvia H. Allred
October 2011 General Conference

Moroni 7:47-48 • 1 Corinthians 13:4-8,13 • Colossians 3:14

Q: Who do you know who exemplifies the virtue of charity? How have they touched your life and helped you feel God's love?

Q: Sister Allred quoted President Monson, who taught, "Charity is having patience with someone who has let us down. It is resisting the impulse to become offended easily. It is accepting weaknesses and shortcomings. It is accepting people as they truly are. It is looking beyond physical appearances to attributes that will not dim through time. It is resisting the impulse to categorize others" ("Charity Never Faileth"). Considering this definition of the pure love of Christ, who needs your charity today?

Sharing His Light

Study 3

DAILY READING:

"Be an Example of the Believers," by Mary N. Cook
October 2012 General Conference

Articles of Faith 1:13 • 1 Timothy 4:12 • Proverbs 31:10

Q: Who in your life is a good example to you of a "believer?" How does that person share the light of Christ? Which of their characteristics are you inspired to develop within yourself?

Q: In what ways can you more clearly be an "example of the believers" to the people around you: your children, grandchildren, roommates, friends, and strangers? What are the habits you'd like to establish in your life that will help you?

Sharing His Light

Study 4

DAILY READING:

"That They May See," by Bonnie H. Cordon
April 2020 General Conference

3 Nephi 12:16 • 3 Nephi 18:24 • Doctrine & Covenant 123:11-13

Q: Think of someone in spiritual need who could use your help right now. How can you meet that person where they are and shine the light of Christ on their path so they can see how to access His enabling power?

Q: Sometimes we may feel that our own light is dim, and wonder how we can possibly share what we have with others when it feels so little. Sister Cordon reminds us that "[Christ] will bring the light if we will just point others to Him." In what ways can you do this, even when you feel your own light isn't shining very bright? How does the light in you grow as you share it with others?

Sharing His Light

Study 5

DAILY READING:

"Sharing Your Light," by Neill F. Marriott
October 2014 General Conference

Mosiah 3:19 • Alma 37:6 • Doctrine & Covenants 50:24

Q: What are the small and simple habits in your life that are strengthening your own faith and that of your family? How can you share those things with others?

Q: In what ways can you dig deeper in your study and understanding of the gospel? What can you do to take your study "to the next level"?

Invitation:

Study "The Living Christ" this next week and look for things you haven't noticed before. Make a list of ways you can change to become more like Jesus Christ.

Notes

Moving Forward

I presume we've all been there—we read an impactful book, we attend a life-changing conference, we listen to a soul-stirring speech or sermon. We walk away feeling changed. We leave the experience, whatever it was, with a great desire to be different in some way. I have felt it many times. I know well the high that comes after my spirit has been touched and I've recognized a truth that I desire to implement into my life.

I also know the let-down that seems to show up a few days later when life just continues to move quickly by, when laundry piles up, when our schedules seem overwhelming, when our time is consumed each day with family, and appointments, and obligations. I know what it's like to long to be back in that space—the space where my cup was being filled and my heart was feeling impressions and my motivation was high.

How do we keep that feeling? How do we implement, in a sustainable way, the thoughts and impressions that have come to us during those times of spiritual fulfillment? How do we create forward motion? How can we use the experiences we've had with the Spirit and really, truly allow them to change us?

Our young people are being taught a beautiful practice to practice, and it's being used in youth conferences around the globe. It's called "reflect and review." These teenagers are learning the importance of pondering over and reflecting on the feelings they had from that day, the impressions they received, the inspiration they felt, and are encouraged to write it down. Once written down, they're taught to review it and create goals- actionable measures that will allow them to use what they were given and grow as they move forward in life.

Elder Richard G. Scott once taught, "Write down in a secure place the important things you learn from the Spirit. You will find that as you write down precious impressions, often more will come. Also, the knowledge you gain will be available throughout your life." (Richard G. Scott, "To Acquire Knowledge and the Strength to Use It Wisely," Ensign, June 2002, 32.)

The following few pages will allow you to "reflect on and review" the things you learned as you worked through this study guide. It is my hope that as you've studied, you've received multiple promptings and impressions about your divine identity, your life, what you need to focus on, habits to create, things to stop doing, your personal mission, and so on. I hope you've seen patterns. I hope you've felt a desire to grow and change through the hours you've spent in this book.

The Savior of the world knows you intimately. He understands your background, your lived experiences, your personality, and your current circumstances. He knows what you can become. He knows what possibilities and opportunities await you. As you think back on the insights that you've gleaned and look forward to setting some new goals, I promise that the Lord will help you accomplish the things He has put into your mind and heart.

Move forward with faith, dear friend. You were created for great things.

Sincerely,
Rachel

Reflect and Review

1. Where are you in the process of personal conversion? And what steps can you take to deepen that conversion? Where is the most beneficial place you could give your time to strengthen your conversion to Jesus Christ?

2. Strengthening our faith involves fortifying our hope and trust in the Savior. In what ways can you increase your hope and your trust in Him and His promises?

3. Who were you created to become? What steps can you take to stop cycles of comparison or self-doubt as you seek to grow into your divine potential?

4. We each have important work to do on this earth. We each have things that we are called to do. Do you know what your unique mission is? What are you drawn to? What topics or experiences tend to surface again and again in your life? How can you tap into those things to help you discover your divine purpose?

5. How do your unique spiritual gifts allow you to fulfill your calling as a disciple of Jesus Christ? What are some of the traits you'd like to have, but feel you are currently lacking? How can you allow the Savior to help you develop those traits and turn your weaknesses into strengths?

6. In what ways does sharing the light of Christ with others come naturally to you? In our unique spiritual creation, we were each blessed with different tendencies—ways that projecting His light is easy for us. Perhaps it's through music, perhaps it's by being a good listener, perhaps it's by always knowing the right words to say, perhaps it's by easily befriending others. Determine where you feel most natural in your discipleship, then strive to strengthen those traits, as well as look for other ways you can share His light with the world that feel true to your unique self.

"We need women who have a bedrock
understanding of the doctrine of Christ and
who will use that understanding to teach and
help raise a sin-resistant generation.
We need women who can detect deception in
all of its forms.
We need women who know how to access the
power that God makes available
to covenant keepers and who express
their beliefs with confidence and charity.
We need women who have the courage and
vision of our Mother Eve.
My dear sisters, nothing is more crucial to
your eternal life than your own conversion."

—Russell M. Nelson

References

Ann M. Dibb, *Be of a Good Courage*, General Conference (Salt Lake City: The Church of Jesus Christ of Latter-day Saints), April 2010, Gospel Library App.

Anne C. Pingree, *Seeing the Promises Afar Off*, General Conference (Salt Lake City: The Church of Jesus Christ of Latter-day Saints), October 2003, Gospel Library App.

——, *Knowing the Lord's Will for You*, General Conference (Salt Lake City: The Church of Jesus Christ of Latter-day Saints), October 2005, Gospel Library App.

Bonnie H. Cordon, *Trust in the Lord and Lean Not*, General Conference (Salt Lake City: The Church of Jesus Christ of Latter-day Saints), April 2017, Gospel Library App.

—, *That They May See*, General Conference (Salt Lake City: The Church of Jesus Christ of Latter-day Saints), April 2020, Gospel Library App.

Bonnie L. Oscarson, *Be Ye Converted*, General Conference (Salt Lake City: The Church of Jesus Christ of Latter-day Saints), October 2013, Gospel Library App.

——, *The Needs before Us*, General Conference (Salt Lake City: The Church of Jesus Christ of Latter-day Saints), October 2017, Gospel Library App.

Camille N. Johnson, *Invite Christ to Author Your Story*, General Conference (Salt Lake City: The Church of Jesus Christ of Latter-day Saints), October 2021, Gospel Library App.

Carol F. McConkie, *Live According to the Words of the Prophets*, General Conference (Salt Lake City: The Church of Jesus Christ of Latter-day Saints), October 2014, Gospel Library App.

Chieko Okazaki, *Cat's Cradle of Kindness*, General Conference (Salt Lake City: The Church of Jesus Christ of Latter-day Saints), April 1993, Gospel Library App.

Christina B. Franco, *The Joy of Unselfish Service*, General Conference (Salt Lake City: The Church of Jesus Christ of Latter-day Saints), October 2018, Gospel Library App.

David B. Haight, "A Time for Preparation," *Ensign*, The Church of Jesus Christ of Latter-Day Saints, Salt Lake City, UT, November 1991.

Elaine S. Dalton, *Press Forward and Be Steadfast*, General Conference (Salt Lake City: The Church of Jesus Christ of Latter-day Saints), April 2003, Gospel Library App.

——, *Believe!*, General Conference (Salt Lake City: The Church of Jesus Christ of Latter-day Saints), April 2004, Gospel Library App.

——, *He Knows You by Name*, General Conference (Salt Lake City: The Church of Jesus Christ of Latter-day Saints), April 2005, Gospel Library App.

——, *Stay on the Path*, General Conference (Salt Lake City: The Church of Jesus Christ of Latter-day Saints), April 2007, Gospel Library App.

Gordon B. Hinckley, "I Believe," *New Era*, The Church of Jesus Christ of Latter-Day Saints, Salt Lake City, UT, September 1996.

Jean A. Stevens, *Fear Not, I Am with Thee*, General Conference (Salt Lake City: The Church of Jesus Christ of Latter-day Saints), April 2014, Gospel Library App.

Joy D. Jones, *For Him*, General Conference (Salt Lake City: The Church of Jesus Christ of Latter-day Saints), October 2018, Gospel Library App.

——, *An Especially Noble Calling*, General Conference (Salt Lake City: The Church of Jesus Christ of Latter-day Saints), April 2020, Gospel Library App.

Julie B. Beck, *And upon the Handmaids in Those Days Will I Pour Out My Spirit*, General Conference (Salt Lake City: The Church of Jesus Christ of Latter-day Saints), April 2010, Gospel Library App.

Kathleen H. Hughes, *What Greater Goodness Can We Know: Christlike Friends*, General Conference (Salt Lake City: The Church of Jesus Christ of Latter-day Saints), April 2005, Gospel Library App.

Linda K. Burton, *Certain Women*, General Conference (Salt Lake City: The Church of Jesus Christ of Latter-day Saints), April 2017, Gospel Library App.

Margaret D. Nadauld, *The Joy of Womanhood*, General Conference (Salt Lake City: The Church of Jesus Christ of Latter-day Saints), October 2000, Gospel Library App.

——, *A Woman of Faith*, General Conference (Salt Lake City: The Church of Jesus Christ of Latter-day Saints), October 2002, Gospel Library App.

Mary N. Cook, *Be an Example of the Believers*, General Conference (Salt Lake City: The Church of Jesus Christ of Latter-day Saints), October 2012, Gospel Library App.

Michelle D. Craig, *Divine Discontent*, General Conference (Salt Lake City: The Church of Jesus Christ of Latter-day Saints), October 2018, Gospel Library App.

——, *Spiritual Capacity*, General Conference (Salt Lake City: The Church of Jesus Christ of Latter-day Saints), October 2019, Gospel Library App.

Neal A. Maxwell, *Swallowed Up in the Will of the Father*, General Conference (Salt Lake City: The Church of Jesus Christ of Latter-day Saints), October 1995, Gospel Library App.

——, "Becoming a Disciple," *Ensign*, The Church of Jesus Christ of Latter-Day Saints, Salt Lake City, UT, June 1996.

——, *The Soul's Sincere Desire*, General Conference (Salt Lake City: The Church of Jesus Christ of Latter-day Saints), October 2016, Gospel Library App.

Neill F. Marriott, *Sharing Your Light*, General Conference (Salt Lake City: The Church of Jesus Christ of Latter-day Saints), October 2014, Gospel Library App.

Russell M. Nelson, "Christ is Risen; Faith in Him Will Move Mountains," *Liahona*, The Church of Jesus Christ of Latter-Day Saints, Salt Lake City, UT, May 2021.

Sheri L. Dew, *We Are Women of God*, General Conference (Salt Lake City: The Church of Jesus Christ of Latter-day Saints), October 1999, Gospel Library App.

——. *Stand Tall and Stand Together*, General Conference (Salt Lake City: The Church of Jesus Christ of Latter-day Saints), October 2000, Gospel Library App.

Silvia H. Allred, *Charity Never Faileth*, General Conference (Salt Lake City: The Church of Jesus Christ of Latter-day Saints), October 2011, Gospel Library App.

Susan H. Porter, *God's Love: The Most Joyous to the Soul*, General Conference (Salt Lake City: The Church of Jesus Christ of Latter-day Saints), October 2021, Gospel Library App.

"The Living Christ: The Testimony of the Apostles of The Church of Jesus Christ of Latter-day Saints," *Ensign*, April 2000, 2.

Thomas S. Monson, "Charity Never Faileth," *Ensign*, The Church of Jesus Christ of Latter-Day Saints, Salt Lake City, UT, November 2010.

True to the Faith: A Gospel Reference, 1st ed., The Church of Jesus Christ of Latter-day Saints, Salt Lake City, UT, 2004, 41.

Seeking Diligently